CW00688589

Our Loving Father

Feeling God's Embrace

Six Studies for Groups or Individuals
with Notes for Leaders

Jack Kuhatschek
Foreword by J. I. Packer

ZondervanPublishingHouse
Grand Rapids, Michigan

A Division of HarperCollins*Publishers*

OUR LOVING FATHER: *Feeling God's Embrace*
Copyright © 1994 by Jack Kuhatschek

Requests for information should be addressed to:
Zondervan Publishing House
Grand Rapids, MI 49530

ISBN 0-310-48291-7

Edited by Jack Kuhatschek
Cover design by Mark Veldheer
Cover photograph by David Woodfall
Interior design by Mark Veldheer & Art Jacobs

Printed in the United States of America

98 99 / ❖ DP / 10 9 8 7 6 5 4

Contents

Foreword

One big difference between our current culture and that of a century ago is that the Victorians saw life in terms of roles, while we see it in terms of relationships. Real life, we say, is a matter of relationships, for roles minimize personal involvement while relationships maximize it.

In saying this, we speak more Christian truth than perhaps we realize. For real life according to the Bible means relating not just to other people but also to the personal God who made us. We live and move and exist in him, and it is both scandalous and impoverishing when we ignore him.

Who is he? The startling truth is that he is a *society*. The Father, Son, and Holy Spirit share with each other an intimate and loving relationship. Yet in the unity of their interpersonal life, they constitute a single divine being. God is they, a society and a team, and they are he, the only God there is.

A mystery? An inexplicable reality? Yes, but a life-giving one. It is our privilege not simply to acknowledge the truth of the Trinity but also to enter into Spirit-sustained relationship with the Father and the Son—a relationship which from one standpoint is *eternal life*, and from another is *knowing God*.

Knowing people involves, first, knowing facts about them and, second, making their acquaintance. How deep our relationship goes depends on how much empathy we have, how many concerns and interests we share, and how much we seek to exalt the one we love. It is the same with knowing God.

The Bible is God's communication to all who hear or read it. Through its varied contents the Triune Lord tells us about himself and calls us to himself. A proper understanding of the Bible will focus at every point on both the information about God and the invitation to know him.

Knowing God Bible Studies are designed to help you achieve this focus. I heartily recommend them. They generate vision, insight, wisdom, and devotion in equal quantities. Use them and you will be blessed.

J. I. Packer

Knowing God Bible Studies

Every Christian desires a deeper, more personal relationship with God. We long to know him better, to feel his presence, and to experience his power in our lives. Jesus himself tells us, "This is eternal life: that they may know you, the only true God, and Jesus Christ, whom you have sent" (John 17:3).

Knowing God Bible Studies can help you build greater intimacy with God. The series explores who God is and how you can know him better. Each guide focuses on a specific attribute of God, such as his love, his faithfulness, or his mercy. The studies are warm and practical and personal—yet they are firmly grounded in Scripture.

The Knowing God series has been field tested in churches across America, representing a wide variety of denominations. This time-intensive process ensures that the guides have solid biblical content, consistent quality, easy-to-use formats, and helpful leader's notes.

Knowing God Bible Studies are designed to be flexible. You can use the guides in any order that is best for you or your group. They are ideal for Sunday-school classes, small groups, one-on-one relationships, or as materials for your quiet times.

Because each guide contains only six studies, you can easily explore more than one attribute of God. In a Sunday-school class, any two guides can be combined for a quarter (twelve weeks), or the entire series can be covered in a year.

Each study deliberately focuses on a limited number of passages, usually only one or two. That allows you to see each passage in its context, avoiding the temptation of prooftexting and the frustration of "Bible hopscotch" (jumping from verse to verse). If you would like to look up additional passages, a Bible concordance will give the most help.

Knowing God Bible Studies help you discover what the Bible says rather than simply telling you the answers. The questions encourage you to think and to explore options rather than merely to fill in the blanks with one-word answers.

Leader's notes are provided in the back of each guide. They show how to lead a group discussion, provide additional information on questions, and suggest ways to deal with problems that may come up in the discussion. With such helps, someone with little or no experience can lead an effective study.

SUGGESTIONS FOR INDIVIDUAL STUDY

1. Begin each study with prayer. Ask God to help you understand the passage and to apply it to your life.

2. A good modern translation, such as the New International Version, the New American Standard Bible, or the New Revised Standard Version, will give you the most help. Questions in this guide, however, are based on the New International Version.

3. Read and reread the passage(s). You must know what the passage says before you can understand what it means and how it applies to you.

4. Write your answers in the space provided in the study guide. This will help you to clearly express your understanding of the passage.

5. Keep a Bible dictionary handy. Use it to look up any unfamiliar words, names, or places.

SUGGESTIONS FOR GROUP STUDY

1. Come to the study prepared. Careful preparation will greatly enrich your time in group discussion.

2. Be willing to join in the discussion. The leader of the group will not be lecturing but will encourage people to discuss what they have learned in the passage. Plan to share what God has taught you in your individual study.

3. Stick to the passage being studied. Base your answers on the verses being discussed rather than on outside authorities such as commentaries or your favorite author or speaker.

4. Try to be sensitive to the other members of the group. Listen attentively when they speak, and be affirming whenever you can. This will encourage more hesitant members of the group to participate.

5. Be careful not to dominate the discussion. By all means participate! But allow others to have equal time.

6. If you are the discussion leader, you will find additional suggestions and helpful ideas in the leader's notes at the back of the guide.

Introducing Our Loving Father

My children love to sit in my lap. They snuggle up close to me, leaning against my chest, and I wrap my arms gently but firmly around them. To them I am strong and powerful. Yet they aren't afraid of that strength but rather feel protected and comforted by it. After all, I am their father. And holding and hugging is one of the ways I express my love for them.

In the Parable of the Lost Son, Jesus describes the Father as one who loves us deeply, who runs to meet us even after we have wounded and rejected him, and who throws his strong arms around us and kisses us (Luke 15:20). Is it any wonder that the apostle John confesses his amazement when he writes, "How great is the love the Father has lavished on us, that we should be called children of God! And that is what we are!" (1 John 3:1).

Yet many Christians do not view God or themselves in that way. We live in a day of broken homes and blended families. Some children rarely see their real fathers. Others are emotionally or physically abused. For them the word *father* does not bring to mind images of love and acceptance but rather makes them think of someone who yelled at them, beat them, or made them feel worthless and ashamed.

Even if you grew up in a "good" family, you may not feel fully loved and accepted by God. If you struggle with low self-esteem, you may wonder how *anyone*—much less God—could really know you and still accept you. Or God may seem distant, uninvolved in the daily affairs of your life. You know the Bible teaches that God loves you, but his love seems more like a cold belief in your mind than a warm experience in your heart.

In this study guide, we will explore not only what Scripture says about God's love but also how we can experience his love to the fullest. The Bible presents an astounding portrait of our heavenly Father. The six passages we will look at tell us that he will always love us, he will never leave us, he takes care of us, he comforts us, he disciplines us, and he wants us to be like him.

If you approach each passage with a genuine desire not only to learn about the Father but also to know him better, then you will not be disappointed. The Bible promises, "Come close to God and he will come close to you" (James 4:8 Phillips). As you seek to come close to our loving Father, may you feel his strong embrace.

Jack Kuhatschek

1

He Will Always Love Us

Luke 15:11-32

A young child was sitting in church one day, listening to the pastor preach on the attributes of God.

"God is holy and just," said the pastor.

"God is omnipotent," he added.

"God is also eternal."

At that point, the child protested in a loud voice, "God is not a *turtle!*"

We don't always understand God's attributes, especially his love. In Luke 15, Jesus tells the Parable of the Lost Son. The story vividly illustrates how eagerly God forgives us and how deeply he loves us.

1. Why is it often hard for people to accept the fact that God loves them?

2. Read Luke 15:11–32. What is unusual about the younger son's request (vv. 11–12)?

3. In what specific ways does Jesus emphasize the younger son's rebellion and decline (vv. 13–16)?

4. What evidence do you see in verses 17–20 that the son truly "came to his senses"?

5. Have you ever felt unworthy to be called a child of God? Why?

6. What do the details in verse 20 reveal about your heavenly Father's love for you?

In what ways have you recently experienced his compassion and tender embrace?

7. The father doesn't even wait for his son to finish his rehearsed speech (v. 21). What do you think "the best robe," "ring," "sandals," and "fattened calf" symbolized in that culture (vv. 22–23)?

8. Why do you think the father's view of his son is so different from the son's view of himself?

9. In what ways do you think your heavenly Father views you differently than you view yourself?

10. The father does not minimize the seriousness of his son's previous actions (v. 24). Nor does Jesus minimize the need for repentance (vv. 7, 10, 17–20). How do these two sober facts give added meaning to the feast and celebration?

11. The older brother's response forms an epilogue to the story. How does the context of the parable (see vv. 1–2) help us understand why the parable doesn't end with verse 27?

12. What sort of religious person today might respond the way the older brother, the Pharisees, and the teachers of the law did?

13. What impresses you about the father's response to the older son's angry outburst (vv. 31–32)?

14. Take time now to thank the Lord for being such a compassionate and forgiving Father.

Memory Verse

But while he was still a long way off, his father saw him and was filled with compassion for him; he ran to his son, threw his arms around him and kissed him. . . . "Let's have a feast and celebrate. For this son of mine was dead and is alive again; he was lost and is found."

Luke 15:20, 23–24

BETWEEN STUDIES

Look up the following passages. How does each one help you to appreciate the Father's love for you?

❑ Romans 5:6–10

❑ Romans 8:31–39

❑ Ephesians 3:17–19

❑ Colossians 2:13–15

Ask the Lord to reveal to you any areas in your life where you need to repent. Come near to God in prayer with the assurance that he will eagerly come near to you (James 4:8).

2

He Will Never Leave Us

Psalm 139

According to Garrison Keillor, author of *Leaving Home*, Florian Krebsbach had to drive his wife, Myrtle, into Minneapolis one day to see a doctor. After they had gone a few miles, they pulled into a truck stop to get some coffee and pie. When they had finished eating,

> they stood up and went and got in the car, then he decided to use the men's room. While he was gone, she went to the ladies' room. And while she was gone, he got in behind the wheel, started up, checked the side mirror, and headed out on the freeway. Who knows how this sort of thing happens, he just didn't notice, his mind was on other things, and Florian is a man who thinks slowly so he won't have to go back and think it over again. He was still thinking about how much he'd miss her if she was gone, how awful he'd feel, how empty the house would be with him lying alone in bed at night . . . and he turned to tell her how much he'd miss her and she wasn't there. The seat was empty. You could have knocked him over with a stick.[1]

There is nothing worse in life than being alone. Of course, we enjoy our moments of solitude (especially if you have kids), but that is different than being truly alone. In Psalm 139, David describes the constant companionship of the One who will never leave us.

1. What are some of the hardships of being truly alone in the world?

2. Read Psalm 139. What statements in verses 1–6 indicate that God's knows you intimately?

3. Like David, why should we view God's intimate knowledge of us as "wonderful" and "lofty" (v. 6)?

4. In verses 7–12 David imagines himself fleeing from God's presence. What extremes does he go to in order to escape from God?

5. What does David's exhausting imaginary journey reveal to him about God?

How is David's discovery much more personal than some abstract concept of God's omnipresence (v. 10)?

6. In what ways do we tend to run from God or hide from his presence?

7. Do you feel comforted or threatened by the fact that you cannot escape from God? Explain.

8. God knows us and will never leave us because he created us (vv. 13–18). What words and phrases in these verses reveal his careful and loving attention to every detail of your creation?

9. Do you view yourself as "fearfully and wonderfully made"—God's masterpiece? Why or why not?

10. Why do you think David's vision of God makes him hate evil and motivates him to purify his life (vv. 19–24)?

11. How do you respond to the fact that God created you, knows you intimately, and will never leave you?

12. What can you do to come closer to the One who is so close to you?

Memory Verse

O LORD, you have searched me and you know me. You know when I sit and when I rise; you perceive my thoughts from afar. You discern my going out and my lying down; you are familiar with all my ways.

Psalm 139:1–3

BETWEEN STUDIES

Take time today and each day this week to be alone with God and to enjoy his presence. Begin your time by rereading one of the four sections of Psalm 139 (vv. 1–6, 7–12, 13–18, 19–24).

What do you learn about your heavenly Father from each part of the psalm? How does it make you feel to know he is actively involved in your life?

Each day, think of an appropriate way to respond to God in worship, thanksgiving, and obedience.

Note

1. *Leaving Home* (New York: Viking, 1987), pp. 56–57.

3

He Takes Care of Us

Psalm 103

W hen my daughter, Katie, was fifteen months old, we thought she might have cystic fibrosis, a disease that affects the respiratory system and can be fatal. The doctor observed symptoms in her that made him want to test for the disease.

While my wife and I waited in anguish for the test results, I realized for the first time the intensity of my love for Katie. I didn't want anything to hurt my child, and I felt agony over the thought of her suffering. We prayed for her constantly and asked friends to do the same. When the crisis was over and the test results were negative, I felt an enormous relief!

God's care for us is far greater than my care for Katie. He is the first and original Father, and all parental love is merely a small reflection of the care he shows his children. Psalm 103 describes some of the amazing qualities of that care.

1. In what ways do parents display some of the best qualities of love toward their children?

2. Read Psalm 103. What words and phrases reveal the mood of this psalm?

3. Verses 1–5 describe some of David's personal reasons for praising the Lord. What good things has God done for him?

4. What are some specific ways you have experienced God's forgiveness? healing? redemption? love and compassion (vv. 3–4)?

5. How has he satisfied your desires with good things (v. 5)?

6. What excellent qualities of God does David focus on in verses 6–12?

7. If our lives are comfortable, it is easy to skip over verse 6: "The LORD works righteousness and justice for all the oppressed." In a world filled with famine, homelessness, and human-rights violations, what does this verse tell us about God's activity and character?

8. How do verses 8–12 strain to describe the magnitude of God's love for us and the vastness of his forgiveness?

How can these verses reassure us when we feel condemned by God rather than loved?

9. In what ways can a father's compassion for his children (v. 13) give us insight into God's compassion for us?

10. Which of our human frailties evoke God's compassion (vv. 14–16)?

11. If we fear God, how does his love triumph over our frailties (vv. 17–18)?

12. Do you see evidence of a healthy "fear" (reverence, respect, and awe) of God in your life? Explain.

13. The psalm concludes with David acting like a choirmaster, summoning the various sections of a heavenly and earthly choir (vv. 20–22). What qualities of God in this psalm make you want to join this hallelujah chorus?

Take a few minutes to do so now.

Memory Verse

Praise the LORD, O my soul; all my inmost being, praise his holy name. Praise the LORD, O my soul, and forget not all his benefits.

Psalm 103:1–2

BETWEEN STUDIES

Take a piece of paper and write at the top: "God's Benefits to Me." Now give several specific examples under the headings David mentions. For example, what are some of the sins in your life that God has forgiven and forgotten? What diseases or illnesses has he healed? What "pits" has he redeemed you from? In what specific ways has he shown you love and compassion? What good things has he given you to satisfy your desires? Use these specific items as the basis for a time of worship, thanksgiving, and praise.

4

He Comforts Us

2 Corinthians 1:3-11

When I was in first grade, the teacher spanked me in front of the entire class. Even now the spank doesn't seem quite fair. She had left the room for a few minutes while we read our "Dick and Jane" books. I was showing off to the kids in my group by reading upside down. I thought it was a pretty neat trick—something that deserved recognition and praise, not a spank. But the teacher didn't see it that way.

When we went out for recess that day, none of my classmates would play with me. Most of them had never seen anyone spanked in school before, and I suppose I seemed like a criminal to them. Finally, the "fat kid" in our class, Bobby Cummings, came over to comfort me in my misery. (He, too, knew what it was like to be rejected.) Even though that was thirty-seven years ago, I have never forgotten his kindness.

In 2 Corinthians 1:3–11 Paul describes our heavenly Father as "the God of all comfort." The passage describes not only how God comforts us but also how we can share his comfort with others.

1. The Bible repeatedly talks about the benefits of suffering (see, for example, Rom. 5:3–5; James 1:2–4; and 1 Peter 1:5–7). Yet if a course were offered entitled "Suffering 101," why do you think so few Christians would enroll?

2. Read 2 Corinthians 1:3–11. What do we learn about God from Paul's rich description in verse 3?

3. When have you experienced God's compassion and comfort during a time of suffering?

4. The word "comfort" appears nine times in verses 3–7. How are suffering and comfort intertwined in the lives of Christians?

Why does God comfort us in the troubles we face as Christians?

5. Why do you think people who have received comfort—either from friends or from God—are best able to comfort others?

6. In what specific ways might we be able to extend God's comfort to others who are suffering?

7. The words "troubles," "sufferings," and "hardships" also appear repeatedly in this passage. What kinds of suffering do you think Paul has in mind? Explain.

8. Do you think the promises about God's comfort apply only to sufferings for Christ or also to other kinds of suffering? Explain.

9. Why do you think Paul wanted the Corinthians to be aware of the hardships he suffered in the province of Asia (vv. 8–11)?

10. In what ways did that extreme suffering prove extremely valuable in Paul's spiritual growth and understanding?

11. How does Paul's experience in Asia help us understand why God sometimes allows us to get to the end of our resources before he delivers us?

12. Why is prayer a vital resource during our own sufferings or when those we love are suffering (vv. 10–11)?

13. In what areas do you or someone you know need God's comfort and deliverance? Bring these concerns now to God in prayer.

Memory Verse

Praise be to the God and Father of our Lord Jesus Christ, the Father of compassion and the God of all comfort, who comforts us in all our troubles, so that we can comfort those in any trouble with the comfort we ourselves have received from God.

2 Corinthians 1:3–4

■ BETWEEN STUDIES ■

Spend time reflecting on the ways you have experienced God's comfort and deliverance as a Christian. Thank God for his faithfulness to you through the years.

Now write down one or two people you know who are experiencing hardship or some kind of difficulty. In what specific ways can you show God's comfort to them this week (a note or letter, a phone call, a visit, a small gift)? Make plans to do so and pray that God will express his compassion through you.

5

He Disciplines Us

Hebrews 12:5-13

In the book *Dare to Discipline*, Dr. James Dobson writes:

> Methods and philosophies regarding control of children have
> been the subject of heated debate and disagreement for
> centuries. The pendulum has swept back and forth regularly
> between harsh, oppressive discipline and the unstructured
> permissiveness of the 1950s. It is time that we realize that both
> extremes leave their characteristic scars on the lives of young
> victims, and I would be hard pressed to say which is more
> damaging.[1]

Even well-meaning parents have a difficult time knowing how
to properly discipline their children. Fortunately, our heavenly
Father does not have that problem. He knows exactly what to
do to bring out the best in his children—and to eliminate the
worst. Hebrews 12:5–13 helps us understand why we should
submit to God's discipline, even when it is painful.

1. In what areas of life do you find that the pains of self-discipline are worth the effort? Explain.

2. Read Hebrews 12:5–13. The "word of encouragement" in verses 5–6 is taken from Proverbs 3:11–12. What two unhealthy responses can we have to the Lord's discipline (v. 5)?

   What might cause us to respond to Lord's discipline in one way or the other?

3. Why should the Lord's discipline encourage us rather than discourage us (v. 6)?

4. The Lord associates discipline with love, and punishment with acceptance (v. 6). Why is it hard for us to see it that way?

5. Hardship is a form of discipline (v. 7). What hardship are you currently facing?

How can seeing that hardship as God's discipline enable you to endure it?

6. Why is the absence of God's discipline far worse than the presence of his discipline (vv. 7–8)?

How can these verses help you not to envy those whose lives seem trouble free?

7. The author of Hebrews assumes that we respected our earthly fathers when they disciplined us and that they did what they thought was best (vv. 9–10). Is that assumption true in your case? Explain.

8. Regardless of the way your earthly father disciplined you, why can you feel safe and confident when your heavenly Father disciplines you (vv. 9–10)?

9. Even though discipline isn't much fun at the time, what are some of the goals and benefits of God's discipline (vv. 10–11)?

Why do you think hardship and discipline produce those results?

10. We need the Father's discipline and training because we are lame, with feeble arms and weak knees (vv. 12–13). In what ways can we "strengthen" ourselves and make "level paths" for our feet?

11. Why can the way we respond to God's discipline result either in healing or a serious disability (v. 13)?

Memory Verse

My son, do not make light of the Lord's discipline, and do not lose heart when he rebukes you, because the Lord disciplines those he loves, and he punishes everyone he accepts as a son.

Hebrews 12:5–6

BETWEEN STUDIES

Using the following chart, write down one hardship you are currently facing. What are some of the positive ways you can respond to the Father's discipline in that situation? What are some of the potential benefits you might gain by submitting to God's discipline? What are some of the potential disabilities you might experience if you refuse to accept God's discipline?

Current Hardships	Positive Responses	Potential Benefits	Potential Disabilities

Note

1. James Dobson, *Dare to Discipline* (Wheaton, Ill.: Tyndale House, 1970), 9.

6

He Wants Us to Be Like Him

1 John 3:1-10

People say that my son, Christopher, looks just like me. If you and I were to walk into a room full of children, you would know immediately that he is my child. There is a strong family resemblance.

Just as we expect children to look like their parents, so our heavenly Father expects us to look and act like him. In 1 John 3:1–10, we discover specific ways we are to resemble God and be different from others.

1. In what ways do you look or act like your parents?

2. Read 1 John 3:1–10. How is God's lavish love for us seen in the title and status he has given us (v. 1)?

3. In what sense does the world not know God's children, just as it did not know God's Son (v. 1)?

4. Although we are God's children, John says that "what we will be has not yet been made known" (v. 2). What are some of the things you wish you knew about life after Christ's return?

5. One thing we do know is that when we see Christ in all his purity, "we shall be like him" (v. 2). How does Christ's purity motivate you to purify your life (v. 3)?

6. What are some of the ways that our lives should demonstrate moral and spiritual purity?

7. Many people claim to know God. But according to John, how does our behavior either confirm or refute that claim (vv. 4–6)?

8. Because righteousness is a gift from God and is not based on "works," we sometimes conclude that a genuine Christian might live a very immoral life. How does that kind of thinking lead us astray (vv. 7–8)?

9. Why is it impossible for those who have been "born of God" to continue to sin (v. 9)?

10. Clearly John does not have in mind sinless perfection (see 1:8–9; 2:1–2). What does he mean, then, when he says we "cannot go on sinning"?

11. In what ways do you see a likeness between you and your heavenly Father?

In what specific ways do you wish you were more like him? (Don't just say "in every way"!)

12. John seems to divide the entire world into the children of God and the children of the devil (v. 10). As you look at verses 1–10, what are some of the ways that each family resembles its parent?

The Children of God	The Children of the Devil

13. Thank God for giving you the privilege of being his child. Ask him to help you to reflect his love and purity in practical ways.

Memory Verse

We know that when he appears, we shall be like him, for we shall see him as he is. Everyone who has this hope in him purifies himself, just as he is pure.

1 John 3:2–3

BETWEEN STUDIES

John tells us that love for our brothers and sisters in Christ is one sign of being God's children. Read and reflect on 1 John 4:7–12. How did God reveal his love to us? How does his love set the standard for our loving others? In what specific ways can you show his love to someone today or this week? Ask him for both the opportunity and the strength to reflect his love to that person.

Leader's Notes

Leading a Bible discussion—especially for the first time—can make you feel both nervous and excited. If you are nervous, realize that you are in good company. Many biblical leaders, such as Moses, Joshua, and the apostle Paul, felt nervous and inadequate to lead others (see, for example, 1 Cor. 2:3). Yet God's grace was sufficient for them, just as it will be for you.

Some excitement is also natural. Your leadership is a gift to the others in the group. Keep in mind, however, that other group members also share responsibility for the group. Your role is simply to stimulate discussion by asking questions and encouraging people to respond. The suggestions listed below can help you to be an effective leader.

PREPARING TO LEAD

1. Ask God to help you understand and apply the passage to your own life. Unless that happens, you will not be prepared to lead others.

2. Carefully work through each question in the study guide. Meditate and reflect on the passage as you formulate your answers.

3. Familiarize yourself with the leader's notes for the study. These will help you understand the purpose of the study

and will provide valuable information about the questions in the study.

4. Pray for the various members of the group. Ask God to use these studies to make you better disciples of Jesus Christ.

5. Before the first meeting, make sure each person has a study guide. Encourage them to prepare beforehand for each study.

LEADING THE STUDY

1. Begin the study on time. If people realize that the study begins on schedule, they will work harder to arrive on time.

2. At the beginning of your first time together, explain that these studies are designed to be discussions, not lectures. Encourage everyone to participate, but realize that some may be hesitant to speak during the first few sessions.

3. Read the introductory paragraph at the beginning of the discussion. This will orient the group to the passage being studied.

4. Read the passage aloud. You may choose to do this yourself, or you might ask for volunteers.

5. The questions in the guide are designed to be used just as they are written. If you wish, you may simply read each one aloud to the group. Or you may prefer to express them in your own words. Unnecessary rewording of the questions, however, is not recommended.

6. Don't be afraid of silence. People in the group may need time to think before responding.

7. Avoid answering your own questions. If necessary, rephrase a question until it is clearly understood. Even an eager group will quickly become passive and silent if they think the leader will do most of the talking.

8. Encourage more than one answer to each question. Ask, "What do the rest of you think?" or "Anyone else?" until several people have had a chance to respond.

9. Try to be affirming whenever possible. Let people know you appreciate their insights into the passage.

10. Never reject an answer. If it is clearly wrong, ask, "Which verse led you to that conclusion?" Or let the group handle the problem by asking them what they think about the question.

11. Avoid going off on tangents. If people wander off course, gently bring them back to the passage being considered.

12. Conclude your time together with conversational prayer. Ask God to help you apply those things that you learned in the study.

13. End on time. This will be easier if you control the pace of the discussion by not spending too much time on some questions or too little on others.

Many more suggestions and helps are found in the book *Leading Bible Discussions* (InterVarsity Press). Reading it would be well worth your time.

STUDY ONE	*He Will Always Love Us*

LUKE 15:11–32

Purpose: To understand how eagerly God forgives us and how deeply he loves us.

Question 1 Every study begins with a "warm-up question," which is discussed *before* reading the passage. A warm-up question is designed to do three things.

First, it helps to break the ice. Because a warm-up question doesn't require any knowledge of the passage or any special preparation, it can get people talking and can help them to feel more comfortable with each other.

Second, a warm-up question can motivate people to study the passage at hand. At the beginning of the study, people in the group aren't necessarily ready to jump into the world of the Bible. Their minds may be on other things (their kids, a problem at work, an upcoming meeting) that have nothing to do with the study. A warm-up question can capture their interest and draw them into the discussion by raising important issues related to the study. The question becomes a bridge between their personal lives and the answers found in Scripture.

Third, a good warm-up question can reveal where people's thoughts or feelings need to be transformed by Scripture. That is why it is important to ask the warm-up question *before* reading the passage. The passage might inhibit the spontaneous, honest answers people might have given, because they feel compelled to give biblical answers. The warm-up question allows them to compare their personal thoughts and feelings with what they later discover in Scripture.

Question 2 "The father might divide the inheritance (double to the older son; see Dt 21:17) but retain the income from it until his death. But to give a younger son his portion of the inheritance upon request was highly unusual" (*The NIV Study Bible* [Grand Rapids, Mich.: Zondervan, 1985], p. 1569).

Question 3 Jesus emphasizes the younger son's rebellion and decline in several ways. First, the son "squandered his wealth in wild living" (v. 13). He was not only irresponsible with his inheritance but also suffered a severe moral lapse. Second, he got a job feeding pigs. For the Jews, pigs were unclean, so this kind of job would have been detestable. Finally, he was so hungry that he would have eaten the slop served to the pigs! The son had gone from being an heir to becoming the lowliest of servants.

Question 6 The father in this passage reveals many aspects of our heavenly Father's love for us. The fact that the father saw his son "while he was still a long way off" (v. 20) indicates that our heavenly Father watches faithfully for us to return to him when we have rebelled against him. And like the father in this passage, our heavenly Father's immediate response is not anger or resentment over our rebellion; rather he is "filled with compassion" when we repent and return to him. When we have sinned against God, we may feel completely unworthy to be his child (as indeed we are), but he throws his arms around us, kisses us, and feels like throwing a party!

Question 7 *"Best robe . . . ring . . . sandals . . . feast."* Each was a sign of position and acceptance (cf. Gen. 41:42; Zech. 3:4): a long robe of distinction, a signet ring of authority, sandals like a son (slaves went barefoot), and the fattened calf for a special occasion" (*The NIV Study Bible*, 1570).

Question 11 Luke 15:1–2, which are the context of the parable, reveal that the son represents people like the "tax collectors and 'sinners'" that gathered around to hear Jesus. Likewise, the older brother represents people like "the Pharisees and the teachers of the law," who resented the fact that Jesus "welcomes sinners and eats with them." We should be careful, however not to press the analogy too far. Would the Father really say to the Pharisees and teachers of the law, "My son, you are always with me, and everything I have is yours" (15:31)?

<table>
<tr><td>

**STUDY
TWO**

</td><td>

He Will Never Leave Us
PSALM 139

</td></tr>
</table>

Purpose: To discover in Psalm 139 the constant companionship of the One who will never leave us.

Question 2 "The psalmist . . . has come to a new level of relationship with the Lord who knows him through and through: 'you have searched me' . . . 'you know' . . . 'you perceive' (v. 2, or 'you have an understanding of'), 'you discern' (v. 3, or 'you have winnowed me'), and 'you are familiar with.' The Lord knows his every move ('when I sit and when I rise,' v. 2). . . . The divine Judge is . . . also the one in whom the psalmist has found protection. He hedges in his own for the purpose of protection ('behind and before,' v. 5). This thought receives further amplification in v.5b: 'you have laid your hand upon me.' The placement of the divine hand signifies protection and blessing" (Willem A. VanGemeren, *Psalms*, The Expositor's Bible Commentary [Grand Rapids, Mich.: Zondervan, 1991], p. 836).

Question 4 "The impulse to flee from God's face (the literal meaning of thy presence) is as old as the Fall. Admittedly the talk of flight may be a purely literary device to dramatize the fact of God's ubiquity; but there seems to be at least an ambivalent attitude to Him here, like that of a child running from its parent" (Derek Kidner, *Psalms 73–150*, Tyndale Old Testament Commentaries [Downers Grove, Ill.: InterVarsity Press, 1975], p. 464).

Question 8 The words "knit me together" (v. 13) and "I was woven together" suggest "the complex patterns and colors of the weaver or embroiderer" (Kidner, *Psalms,* 446). The psalmist also declares that we are "fearfully and wonderfully made" (v. 14), the masterpiece of the divine Artist. Our Creator not only fashioned us with great skill and artistry, he also ordained all of our days, writing them in his book, before one of them came to be (v. 16). This is not the record of an accountant or bookkeeper; our Father pays loving attention not only to our creation but also to every day of our lives.

Question 10 The idea that the psalmist asks God to "slay the wicked" (v. 19), and that he hates and abhors those who hate the Lord and counts them as his enemies (vv. 21–22) seems contrary to the teachings of Jesus, who taught us to love our enemies and to pray for those who persecute us (Matt. 5:43–48). Yet the psalmist's hatred is not indiscriminate. He so identifies with the Lord that he feels the same righteous indignation that the Lord feels toward those who are under his wrath and judgment because of stubborn rebellion. Although both the Old and New Testaments teach the reality of God's love for sinners, they also teach that divine judgment will ultimately fall on those who do not repent (Matt. 23:33–36; Rom. 2:1–11; Heb. 10:26–31; Jude 5–13).

STUDY THREE	*He Takes Care of Us*
	PSALM 103

Purpose: To reflect on the amazing qualities of God's care as seen in Psalm 103.

Question 1 This question deliberately asks about parents in general rather than "your parents" because some in your group may not have positive feelings or memories about their parents' love.

Question 2 "A hymn to God's love and compassion toward his people. . . . Calls to praise frame the body of the hymn (vv. 1–2, 20–22) and set its tone. The recital of praise falls into two unequal parts: (1) a three-verse celebration of personal benefits received (vv. 3–5) and (2) a 14-verse recollection of God's mercies to his people Israel (vv. 6–19)" (*The NIV Study Bible*, p. 894).

Question 6 "From the specific and personal observations of the Lord's goodness (vv. 3–5), the worshiper reflects on God's concern with the establishment of 'righteousness' in his world and especially in Israel (vv. 7–14). The Lord does not tolerate injustice in the world (cf. 33:4–5). His rule is characterized by 'righteousness' as he rights what is wrong. 'Righteousness' (lit., 'righteous acts,' pl.; cf. Judg. 5:11; Mic. 6:5) relates to two aspects of divine activity: 'salvation' (Isa. 51:6, 8) and 'justice' or vindication (Isa. 63:1, 4). He delivers from evil and oppression (. . . 'justice for all the oppressed'; lit., 'judgments for all the oppressed,' cf. 36:6; 146:7). He also avenges the oppressors" (VanGemeren, *Psalms*, p. 653).

Questions 7–8 In order to describe the magnitude of God's love and forgiveness, the psalmist first takes us outside to show us the vastness of the universe. As we look up into the expanse of the space, he tells us that God's love is as great as that. As we look at the distant horizon from east to west, he tells us that is how far God has removed our transgressions from us.

Next, the psalmist brings us back inside, to the home. There he uses the greatness of an earthly father's compassion for his children to give us a glimpse of the kind of compassion our heavenly Father has for us.

Question 12 We should not confuse fearing the Lord with being frightened of him. In the Bible, "Holy fear . . . is God-given, enabling men to reverence God's authority, obey His commandments, and hate and shun all forms of evil (Je. xxxii. 40; *cf.* Gn. xxii. 12; Heb. v. 7). It is, moreover, the beginning of wisdom (Ps. cxi. 10); the secret of uprightness (Pr. viii. 13); a feature of the people in whom God delights (Ps. cxlvii. 11); and the whole duty of man (Ec. xii. 13)" (*The New Bible Dictionary*, ed. J. D. Douglas [Grand Rapids, Mich.: Eerdmans, 1962], p. 419).

Question 13 As the group looks at these verses, try to get them to use their imagination. "Try to picture the mighty angels in one section of the orchestra, the heavenly hosts (countless multitudes) in another, all other created beings and things in another, and the psalmist standing in the conductor's place. With sweeping gestures, he draws out notes of praise first from one section then another, until the entire creation—including the psalmist—is praising and worshiping the Lord. This is an overpowering scene! . . ."

"Each member of the orchestra is characterized by obedience. The mighty ones *do his bidding* and *obey his word* (v. 20). The heavenly hosts are *servants* who *do his will* (v. 21). Likewise, all his works are under *his dominion*. The assumption is that the psalmist and those whom the Lord has saved are also obedient to him" (Eugene H. Peterson, *Psalms: Prayers of the Heart* [Downers Grove, Ill: InterVarsity Press, 1987], pp. 57–58).

<table>
<tr><td>STUDY
FOUR</td><td>

He Comforts Us
2 CORINTHIANS 1:3–11
</td></tr>
</table>

Purpose: To discover not only how God comforts us but also how we can share his comfort with others.

Question 2 Because this is an observation question, encourage people to quickly identify the facts stated about God in verse 3: He is the God and Father of our Lord Jesus Christ, and he is given the titles of "the Father of compassion" and "the God of all comfort." As a follow-up question, you might ask the group what they think these two titles mean.

Question 4 Suffering and comfort should be closely intertwined in the lives of Christians. We should willingly suffer various kinds of hardship in order to bring comfort and salvation to others. Yet as we suffer, the Father of compassion and the God of all comfort works to comfort us in our afflictions. Our experience of God's comfort then enables us to comfort others who experience sufferings.

Question 6 Help the group to think broadly with this question. Perhaps you should focus first on people who are suffering in your church. Then think about those who are suffering in your community. Finally, explore ways in which you can comfort those who are suffering in other places, such as those who are experiencing severe famine.

Question 8 Paul clearly has in mind suffering for Christ's sake and for the sake of the gospel rather than suffering in general. Yet he does describe the Father as "the God of all comfort" (v. 3). Likewise, our God is "the Father of compassion"—the One who is deeply compassionate by nature. Because these qualities characterize our heavenly Father, it is safe to assume that he also feels compassion when we suffer in other ways and that he will comfort us in those afflictions as well.

Question 11 Throughout the Corinthian epistles, Paul stresses the fact that God uses our weaknesses to demonstrate his power and the glory of the gospel (see 1 Cor. 2:1–5; 4:8–13; 2 Cor. 4:7–12; 6:3–10; 10:1–11; 11:16–33; 12:1–10). Weaknesses and hardships have three effects on us and on our ministry: (1) they keep us from being inflated with pride, making us properly humble before God and others, (2) they make us dependent on God rather than on ourselves, and (3) they become a means through which God's power is demonstrated to us and to others.

STUDY FIVE	*He Disciplines Us*
	HEBREWS 12:5–13

Purpose: To consider why we should submit to God's discipline, even when it is painful.

Question 2. Verses 5–6 are taken from Proverbs 3:11–12. Allen P. Ross describes those verses as follows: "The final specific instruction warns the disciple not to rebel against the Lord's discipline, because it is an evidence of his love. Wisdom literature knows that the righteous do not enjoy uninterrupted blessing; suffering remains a problem to the sages, and this text records one of their solutions (see Scott, *Proverbs/Ecclesiastes*, p. 47). This motivation recalls the language of the Davidic covenant (2 Sam. 7:14; Ps. 89:32–33), which mentions discipline in love. Indeed, it is the father-son relationship that provides insight into the nature of that discipline. These verses are quoted in Hebrews 12:5–6 to show that suffering is a sign of sonship" (*Proverbs*, The Expositor's Bible Commentary [Grand Rapids, Mich.: Zondervan, 1991], p. 918).

Question 4 When suffering and hardship enter our lives, we often feel rejected by God and think that he has let us down. After all, peace and prosperity feel so much more pleasant than suffering—and why wouldn't God want us to be happy and content? But although God ultimately wants us to be happy, his more immediate goals are for us to be holy (see v. 10), and holiness is usually forged in the intense heat of suffering.

Question 6 We would love to have all suffering and hardship removed from our lives permanently, and we envy those who are without troubles. But the author of Hebrews does not see it that way. If our lives are completely free from suffering and hardship, then we may also be free from God's discipline. Yet discipline is one of the identifying marks of being God's children, and the absence of discipline may indicate that we are not really members of his family.

Questions 7–8 In this day of child abuse, you need to realize that some members of your group may have been mistreated by their parents, and they may have very unpleasant memories of discipline. For such people it is important to stress that God is not like earthly fathers, who may discipline us in the wrong way or for the wrong reasons. We can always trust in the fact that our heavenly Father disciplines us for our good, that we "may share in his holiness" (v. 10).

Question 11 Those who have physical injuries often need physical therapy. During such therapy, they are often asked by the doctor or trainer to do exercises that will strengthen the injury, and sometimes the therapy is painful. Those who willingly submit to the therapy will see progress and eventual healing. Those who avoid the therapy because of the pain and hard work run the risk of having their injury become a permanent disability. The same is true with those areas of our lives that are spiritually "lame" and need the Father's therapy. We must cooperate with him if we want to get better.

He Wants Us to Be Like Him

1 JOHN 3:1–10

Purpose: To discover specific ways we are to resemble God and be different from others.

Question 1 If some members of your group are adopted, they can describe the ways in which they act like their adoptive parents.

Question 2 "The AV translation, 'Behold, what manner of love the Father hath bestowed upon us,' gets nearer than the NIV to the feel of what John wrote here. There is an aorist imperative at the beginning of the verse: 'Look! See!' The force is that we need to take time to contemplate this love and allow its reality to sink down into the depths of our being. It is meant to take our breath away; to startle and amaze us so that we are left gasping, 'What sort of love is this'? The word John uses (*potapos*) originally meant 'of what country?' It is a word that expresses surprise in encountering something foreign, something we are not used to. The disciples use this word in Matthew 8:27, when, amazed by the power of Jesus in stilling the storm on Galilee, they exclaim, 'What kind of man is this? Even the winds and the waves obey him.' He is in a different category from anything we have come across before. And so is the Father's love for us.

It is a love in which he takes all the initiative to make us his children; a love that gives lavishly and freely to those who are utterly undeserving. When we contemplate our sin and rebellion against the background of God's unapproachable light, his total holiness, we begin to sense something of John's wonder that he should ever bother with people like us. Yet the love of God delights to change rebels into children who belong to the family. Not only does he give us his name (*called children of God*, v. 1) but he gives us his status (*now we are children of God*, v. 2). This is no wishful thinking, no legal fiction, but an eternal reality" (David Jackman, *The Message of John's Letters*, The Bible Speaks Today [Downers Grove, Ill.: InterVarsity Press, 1988], p. 81).

Question 7 Throughout John's letter he makes it clear that those who claim to know God must demonstrate the reality of that claim by their conduct. Here the conduct he looks for is their relationship to sin. The person "who keeps on sinning" may claim to know God, but in fact he has neither seen him nor knows him (v. 6). In other words, he does not have a saving knowledge of God.

Does John mean that we must be sinless to demonstrate the reality of our salvation? Although at times his words give that appearance (see, for example, 3:9), he is not speaking of sinless perfection but rather of a changed lifestyle in which sin is no longer dominant, directing the course of a person's life. John is well aware of the fact that believers sin (2:1–2), and if someone claims to be sinless, John says he is not only deceived but also makes God out to be a liar (1:8–10).

Question 8 John warns us, "Do not let anyone lead you astray" (v. 7). Yet throughout church history, people *have* led professing Christians astray by telling them that because salvation is a free gift (which is certainly true), and because true believers are eternally secure (which I also believe is true), it is possible for a genuine Christian to live a life that is characterized by sin and unrighteousness (which, according to John, is *false*). A genuine saving faith will always result in a transformed lifestyle. If there is no transformation, there is no saving faith.

Of course, we must be careful not to set ourselves up as judges and jurors in this matter. The Lord himself is the One who will ultimately decide the validity of our faith (1 Cor. 4:3–5). Even true believers have ups and downs, and not even the most mature Christian lives without sin. Still, John wants us to realize that there are certain "vital signs" that reveal the presence of eternal life, and a life characterized by righteousness is one such sign.

Question 9 Just as natural children resemble their parents, so John says that those who are "born of God" must resemble their heavenly Father—not in physical ways, of course, but in spiritual ways, because they bear his "genetic" likeness. "The picture is of human reproduction, in which the sperm (the Greek for 'seed' is *sperma*) bears the life principle and transfers the paternal characteristics. *cannot go on sinning.* Not a complete cessation of sin, but a life that is characterized by sin" (*The NIV Study Bible*, p. 1911).

NOTES

NOTES

NOTES

NOTES